D0613315

Contenido

Pensar y conversar	4
Hojas	6
Flores	8
Frutos	10
Crecer y cambiar	12
Usar lo que aprendieron	14
Glosario ilustrado	16

arbusto
árbol frutal
flor
hoja

¿Qué plantas ven?
¿Qué partes tienen?

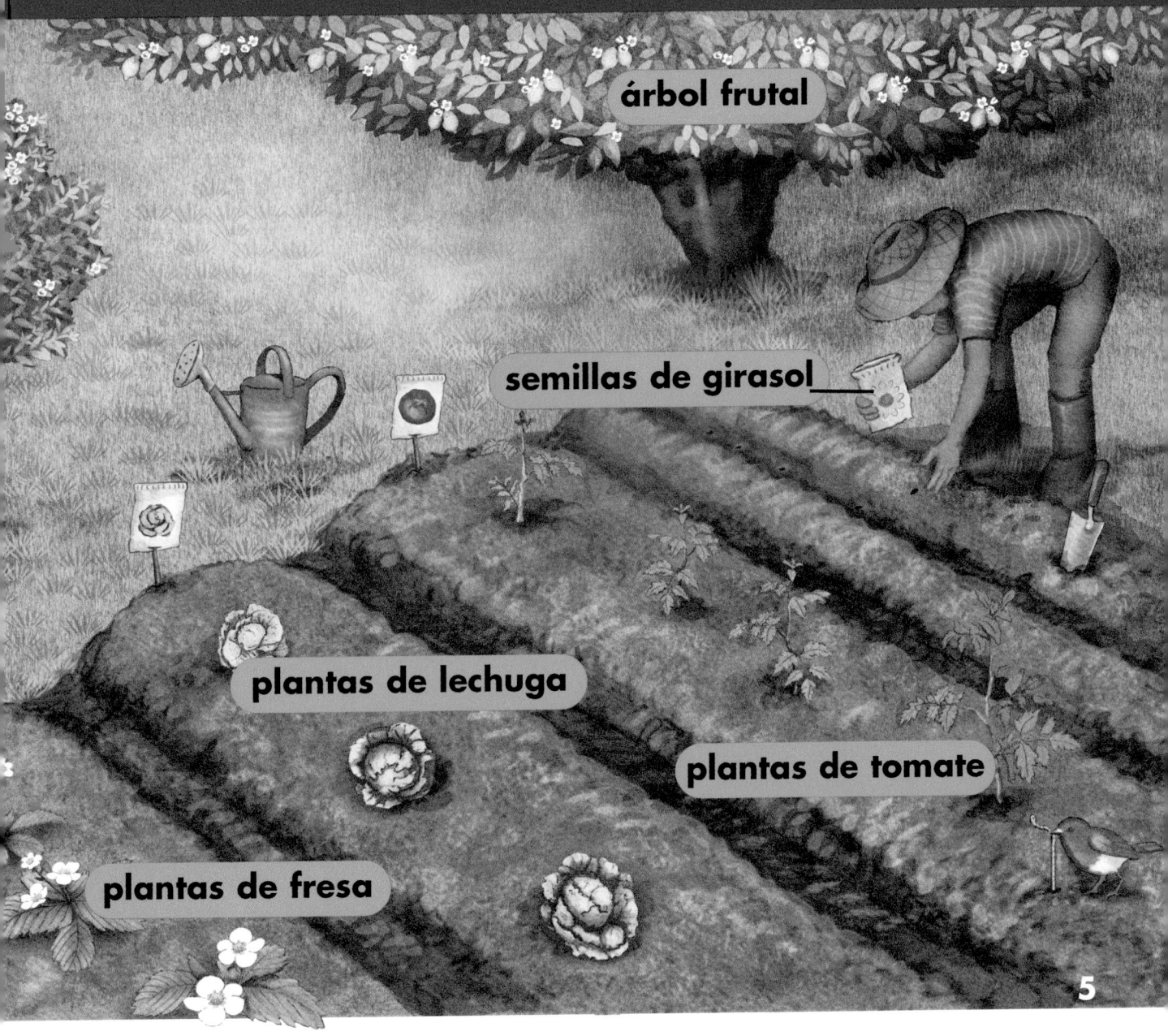

Hojas

La mayoría de las plantas tienen hojas.

Estos árboles tienen hojas.

Estos nenúfares tienen hojas.
Estas plantas tienen hojas.

Flores

Muchas plantas tienen flores.

Esta planta tiene flores.
Este árbol tiene flores.

Frutos

Algunas plantas tienen frutos.

Este arbusto tiene frutos.

Esta planta tiene frutos.

Crecer y cambiar

Todas las plantas crecen y cambian. La mayoría de las plantas salen de semillas.

flores de la fresa

Usar lo que aprendieron

¡Miren las plantas ahora! ¿Qué cambios notan?

cambiar

crecer

flor

fruto

hojas

planta

semilla

Glosario ilustrado

flores

frutos

hojas

plantas

semillas

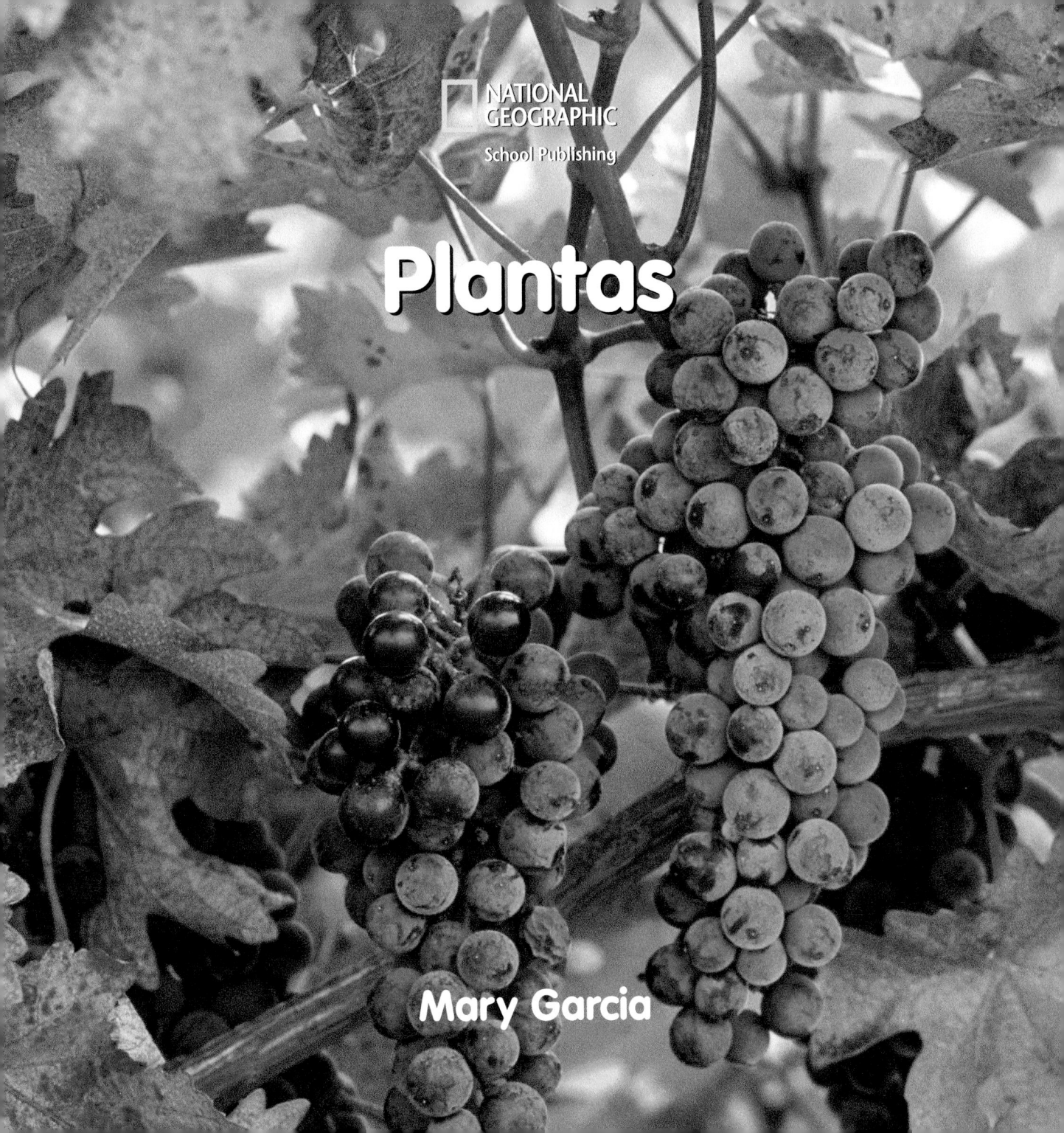

NATIONAL GEOGRAPHIC
School Publishing

Plantas

Mary Garcia

PICTURE CREDITS
Illustrations by Karen Ahlschlager (4–5, 14–15).
Cover, 8 (left), 10 (left), 11 (right), Photolibrary.com; 1, 8 (right), 10 (right), 16 (above left & above right), Getty Images; 2, 6 (all), 7 (all), 9 (inset), 11 (above right), 12 (above right & below right), 13, 16 (center left & center right), APL/Corbis; 9 (left), Zefa Images.

Produced through the worldwide resources of the National Geographic Society, John M. Fahey, Jr., President and Chief Executive Officer; Gilbert M. Grosvenor, Chairman of the Board.

PREPARED BY NATIONAL GEOGRAPHIC SCHOOL PUBLISHING
Ericka Markman, Senior Vice President and President Children's Books and Education Publishing Group; Steve Mico, Senior Vice President and Publisher; Marianne Hiland, Editorial Director; Lynnette Brent, Executive Editor; Michael Murphy and Barbara Wood, Senior Editors; Bea Jackson, Design Director; David Dumo, Art Director; Margaret Sidlowsky, Illustrations Director; Matt Wascavage, Manager of Publishing Services; Sean Philpotts, Production Manager.

SPANISH LANGUAGE VERSION PREPARED BY NATIONAL GEOGRAPHIC SCHOOL PUBLISHING GROUP
Sheron Long, CEO; Sam Gesumaria, President; Fran Downey, Vice President and Publisher; Margaret Sidlosky, Director of Design and Illustrations; Paul Osborn, Senior Editor; Sean Philpotts, Project Manager; Lisa Pergolizzi, Production Manager.

MANUFACTURING AND QUALITY MANAGEMENT
Christopher A. Liedel, Chief Financial Officer; George Bounelis, Vice President; Clifton M. Brown III, Director.

BOOK DEVELOPMENT
Ibis for Kids Australia Pty Limited

SPANISH LANGUAGE TRANSLATION
Tatiana Acosta/Guillermo Gutiérrez

SPANISH LANGUAGE BOOK DEVELOPMENT
Navta Associates, Inc.

Published by the National Geographic Society
Washington, D.C. 20036-4688

Copyright © 2008 National Geographic Society. All rights reserved. Reproduction of the whole or any part of the contents without written permission from the publisher is prohibited. National Geographic, National Geographic School Publishing, National Geographic Windows on Literacy and the Yellow Border are registered trademarks of the National Geographic Society.

ISBN: 978-0-7362-3827-4

Printed in Mexico

Print Number: 03 Print Year: 2023